RIVERS OF
NORTH AMERICA

The **Arkansas** River

by Tom Jackson

Gareth Stevens Publishing
A WORLD ALMANAC EDUCATION GROUP COMPANY

Please visit our web site at: www.garethstevens.com
For a free color catalog describing Gareth Stevens Publishing's list of high-quality
books and multimedia programs, call 1-800-542-2595 (USA) or 1-800-387-3178
(Canada). Gareth Stevens Publishing's fax: (414) 332-3567.

Library of Congress Cataloging-in-Publication Data

Jackson, Tom, 1953–
    The Arkansas River / by Tom Jackson.
        p. cm. — (Rivers of North America)
    Includes bibliographical references and index.
    Contents: Southern river—From source to mouth—The life of the river—Life along the river—
Farms and factories—Places to visit—How rivers form.
    ISBN 0-8368-3752-5 (lib. bdg.)
    1. Arkansas River—Juvenile literature. [1. Arkansas River.] I. Title. II. Series.
  F417.A7J33   2003
  976.7'3—dc21   2003042746

This North American edition first published in 2004 by
Gareth Stevens Publishing
A World Almanac Education Group Company
330 West Olive Street, Suite 100
Milwaukee, Wisconsin 53212 USA

Original copyright © 2004 The Brown Reference Group plc. This U.S. edition copyright © 2004
by Gareth Stevens, Inc.

Author: Tom Jackson
Editor: Tom Jackson
Consultant: Judy Wheatley Maben, Education Director, Water Education Foundation
Designer: Steve Wilson
Cartographer: Mark Walker
Picture Researcher: Clare Newman
Indexer: Kay Ollerenshaw
Managing Editor: Bridget Giles
Art Director: Dave Goodman

Gareth Stevens Editor: Betsy Rasmussen
Gareth Stevens Designer: Melissa Valuch

Picture Credits: Cover: Pueblo Dam, Colorado. (Skyscan: Jim Wark)
Contents: Bison hides at Dodge City, Kansas in 1878.

Key: l–left, r–right, t–top, b–bottom.
Corbis: Bettmann 5b, 16, 21, 27; Richard A. Cooke 29t; Dave G. Houser 15t; David Muench 7, 11t; Carl
& Ann Purcell 4; Charles E. Rotkin 24/25; Joseph Sohm/Vision of America 8/9b; Getty Images: 18; Eddie
Hironaka 13; Bob Thomason 28; Library of Congress: 19; NASA: 8l; National Archives: 14/15, 17, 20;
PhotoDisc: PhotoLink 10; Jeremy Woodhouse 11b; Still Pictures: Jeri Gleiter 22/23; Peter Arnold/John
Kietter 8/9; Peter Arnold/Jim Wark 5t; Norbert Wu 12; TRH Pictures: 26; U.S. Army Corps of Engineers:
25t, 29b

Printed in the United States of America

1 2 3 4 5 6 7 8 9 07 06 05 04 03

Table of Contents

Southern River

The Arkansas is the fourth-longest river in the United States. Its water supplies some of the largest farms in the country, and its main cities are world leaders in high-tech industries.

The Arkansas River flows from the eastern slopes of the Rocky Mountains of Colorado through the vast rolling prairies of the Great Plains, before joining the Mississippi River 1,460 miles (2,348 kilometers) later. The river's name comes from *akansea*—meaning "south wind"— the word used by Native people in the region for the Quapaw people, a Native group that lived along the lower section of the river.

Name Change

People disagree about how to pronounce Arkansas. The first European pioneers in the area were French, and they pronounced the word "Ar-kuhn-saw." However, English-speaking settlers wanted to call it "Ar-kahn-suhs." In 1881, Congress ruled that the state of Arkansas (and the river running through it) should be "Ar-kuhn-saw." In fact, it used to be illegal in that

state to say it the other way. The people of Kansas, a state through which the river also runs, still insist on calling their part of the river the "Ar-kahn-suhs."

River History

The Arkansas River has witnessed many of the important events that made the United States the country it is today. Three hundred years ago, French settlers built the first town west of the Mississippi River near the Arkansas's mouth.

The river and the territory around it have changed ownership many times since then. Soon after this area became part of the United States in 1803, the government began forcing Native people from their land in eastern states. The government sent many of these people down the Arkansas River to Indian Territory, which is now the state of Oklahoma.

Dodge City on the banks of the Arkansas River in Kansas became famous for its "wild west" ways. Gunfights erupted in the city a little more than one hundred years ago, and famous lawmen,

such as Wyatt Earp, had the job of keeping law and order.

Today, the river is still at the center of American life. Its farms produce a huge amount of food, while the cities on its banks are known for making rockets for the space program, jet airplanes, and other high-tech products.

Above right: *The wide Arkansas River makes its way across the forested plain near the river's confluence (meeting) with the Mississippi River.*

Right: *Oil wells, like this one spouting oil from under ground, used to be a common sight near the Arkansas River. Tulsa, Oklahoma, was once the country's main oil city.*

Left: *A historic paddle wheeler steams down the Arkansas River, past the modern skyline of downtown Little Rock, Arkansas.*

1 From Source to Mouth

The Arkansas River flows from the highest peaks in the Rocky Mountains, across the vast grasslands of the Great Plains, and to the lush floodplain of the Mississippi River.

The Arkansas River begins near Leadville in central Colorado. The upper river collects water flowing off the Sawatch Range, close to Mount Elbert, the highest peak in the Rocky Mountains. The Arkansas River flows across four states—Colorado, Kansas, Oklahoma, and Arkansas. The river ends its journey on the border between Arkansas and Mississippi, where it joins the flow of the mighty Mississippi River.

The Arkansas travels 1,460 miles (2,348 km) and is the fourth-longest river in the United States. Through its many smaller tributaries, the Arkansas collects water from a basin of 160,500 square miles (415,695 sq km), which includes parts of New Mexico, Texas, and Missouri.

River Route

The Arkansas River flows roughly southeast on its route to the Mississippi.

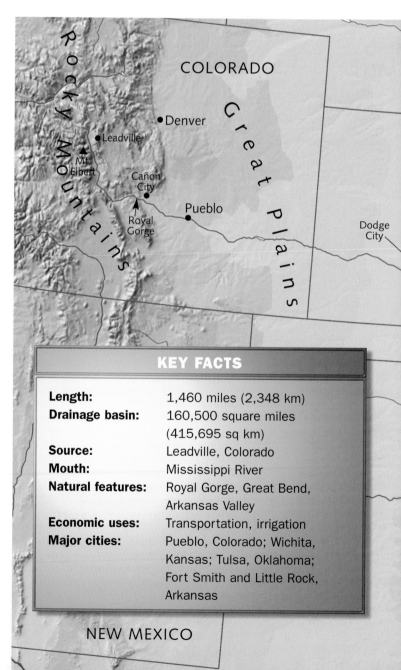

KEY FACTS	
Length:	1,460 miles (2,348 km)
Drainage basin:	160,500 square miles (415,695 sq km)
Source:	Leadville, Colorado
Mouth:	Mississippi River
Natural features:	Royal Gorge, Great Bend, Arkansas Valley
Economic uses:	Transportation, irrigation
Major cities:	Pueblo, Colorado; Wichita, Kansas; Tulsa, Oklahoma; Fort Smith and Little Rock, Arkansas

In its first 125 miles (200 km), the river travels mainly south, plunging 10,000 feet (3,048 meters) down through the rugged mountains to the edge of the rolling prairies of the Great Plains.

A little way upstream of Cañon City, Colorado, the Arkansas River rushes through the Royal Gorge. This canyon has walls more than 1,000 feet (305 m) high, which are only 30 feet (9 m) apart in some places. The world's highest suspension bridge crosses the gorge.

The first large city on the river is Pueblo, Colorado. From there, the Arkansas

Below: *A gnarled cedar tree on Magazine Mountain in the Ouachita Mountains of Arkansas.*

PARKS AND FORESTS

- Comanche National Grassland, Colorado
- Ozark National Forest, Arkansas
- Sequoyah National Wildlife Refuge, Oklahoma

TRIBUTARIES

- Canadian
- Verdigris
- White

NEBRASKA

IOWA

KANSAS

Great Bend

Arkansas River

Wichita

Arkansas City

Verdigris River

Tulsa

Catoosa

Oklahoma City

Muskogee

Canadian River

Eufaula Lake

OKLAHOMA

Ozark Plateau

MISSOURI

Boston Mountains

Arkansas Valley

Forth Smith

Ouachita Mountains

ARKANSAS

White River

Little Rock

Arkansas Post

Pine Bluff

Dumas

Rosedale

Mississippi River

Memphis

TENNESSEE

MISSISSIPPI

ALABAMA

TEXAS

Dallas

LOUISIANA

Shreveport

Jackson

flows through the treeless grasslands of the Great Plains. These prairies stretch all the way from Texas to Canada, and the Arkansas River cuts across them from west to east. The river collects little extra water from the dry grasslands.

After flowing through Dodge City, Kansas, the Arkansas takes a turn to the north and sweeps in a great bend through central Kansas. At the other end of the bend, the river heads southeast again, passing through Wichita, Kansas, before crossing into Oklahoma.

Mountain Pass

Near this point of its course, the river passes into the Ozark Plateau. This rugged region stretches from eastern Oklahoma into northern Arkansas and on into Missouri and Illinois. After the dry and flat grasslands of Kansas, the Arkansas River now picks up a lot of water from many streams flowing off the surrounding hills.

Most of the Arkansas's major tributaries join the river in Oklahoma. Near Tulsa, Oklahoma, the river is joined by its largest tributaries—the Verdigris and Canadian Rivers. Dams on these three rivers have created several mountain reservoirs and made it possible for barges to travel from the Mississippi to Muskogee, Oklahoma.

Crossing into the state of Arkansas at Fort Smith, the river flows southeast

Main image: *Wheat covers the open, rolling land of the Great Plain in eastern Colorado.*

Below left: *A picture taken from a satellite of the Arkansas River Delta.*

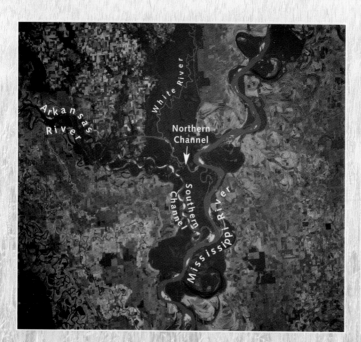

through the wide Arkansas Valley. To the north of the valley loom the Boston Mountains, which edge the Ozark Plateau. To the south, the Ouachita Mountains rise up.

The Arkansas River cuts through these ranges, emerging in central Arkansas near the city of Little Rock, the state capital.

Wide Flow

Swelled by several smaller rivers, the Arkansas now has a powerful flow. Downstream from Little Rock, the Arkansas pours through the Mississippi River's floodplain. In the past, this area was frequently flooded with water from the Arkansas River and the Mississippi itself. Today, the rivers' waters are controlled with drainage ditches and levees (embankments), so serious floods are rare.

Delta Country

Downstream from Pine Bluff, Arkansas, the river contains several large islands. East of the town of Dumas, the Arkansas splits into two separate channels, or distributaries. A river mouth that splits into a triangle like this is called a delta. The northern delta channel is joined by the White River, which flows down from the north of Arkansas. The northern branch is shorter than the southern one, and both reach the Mississippi River a few miles from the town of Rosedale, Mississippi.

Below: *The long Royal Gorge Bridge spans a deep gorge cut by the Arkansas River.*

2 The Life of the River

The wildlife communities living in and beside the Arkansas River change as the river flows from cold mountains to dry grasslands and forested hills.

The Rocky Mountains have a large effect on the climate of the Arkansas. The western section of the region, from its source to Oklahoma, is much drier than the Ozark Plateau and the eastern part of the region in Arkansas.

Rain Shadow

The Rockies prevent much rain from reaching the river's western course. As air blowing from the west rises up over the mountains, it drops nearly all of its rain on the western slopes. The air that flows down the eastern side is much drier and rarely produces rain. Mountain ranges that block rain like this cast what is called a rain shadow.

The western Arkansas River is in a rain shadow, and this has a great effect on the plants and animals that live there. Without heavy rain, the soil is too

Left: *A prairie dog takes a look out of its burrow on the Great Plains. The rodents share burrows called towns.*

ARKANSAS RIVER SHINER

As its name suggests, the Arkansas River shiner, a fish, was unique to the Arkansas River. Today, this small species is extremely rare. This is due mainly to changes in the river's current, caused by reservoirs and dams that damage the riverbed where the shiners live and breed.

About twenty years ago, however, a fisher accidentally introduced some shiners into the Pecos River, which flows through New Mexico and Texas. Now shiners are thriving in the Pecos River. Conservationists are collecting young shiners from the Pecos, raising them in captivity, and releasing them into the Arkansas River in the hope that their population will grow again.

Right: *The Pecos River in New Mexico. Unlike the Arkansas River, the Pecos still has many shallow sandy areas along its banks that river shiners can live in.*

dry for trees to grow in this area. A vast prairie, or grassland, grows instead of forest. There are two hundred kinds of grasses on the prairies of Colorado and Kansas. Kansas is also famous for its sunflowers, which grow well in the region's bright sunshine.

Mountain Streams

Once the river turns south into Oklahoma and on into Arkansas, it enjoys a much

Above: *The sunflower is the state flower of Kansas.*

SALT IN THE WATER

Scientists have discovered that Arkansas River water is very salty. This is because a great deal of river water is sprayed onto fields in Colorado and Kansas. Some of the water evaporates (turns to vapor) in the heat—especially during periods of drought. As the water evaporates, the minerals dissolved in what is left become more concentrated, similar to the way a cooking sauce thickens when the water in it boils away.

This salty water trickles into the ground and eventually back into the river. The water also gets into groundwater that is used to supply homes and factories. This water is six times saltier than normal drinking water.

Below: *A long sprinkler system pours river water onto a field in Colorado.*

wetter climate. The river is swelled by mountain streams that collect rainwater falling on the Ozark Plateau. This rain creates a completely different habitat. Forests of ash, elm, hickory, and maple trees cover the slopes of the Arkansas River Valley and parts of the floodplain closer to the Mississippi.

Prairie and Forest

The animals living on the open prairie are very different from those in the forests and hills beside the eastern part of the river.

Perhaps the most famous prairie animal is the American bison, or buffalo, which once wandered over the plains in enormous herds. In the nineteenth century, however, these animals were hunted to near extinction. Today, a few thousand bison live in protected reserves.

Many other prairie animals still live beside the river, including prairie dogs and armadillos. Prairie dogs are burrowing animals that live in large groups. They eat grasses and small insects.

Armadillos are armored animals that feed on insects and worms.

A large area of the prairie is used for growing food. The farmers sow crops of edible grasses, such as wheat, barley, and rye. Water from the Arkansas River is used to irrigate the dry land of the Great Plains.

A different set of animals lives in the river's forests and hills. These include mink, elk, opossums, raccoons, and white-tailed deer. Unlike prairie dogs, most forest animals live alone, hiding among the thick plant cover. Brown bears are sometimes seen in the hills of Arkansas. Because of this, Arkansas is known as the Bear State.

Air and Water

In the air above the river, ospreys and eagles search for fish and small rodents on the banks, while curlews wade in the shallow marsh areas snapping up snails and worms. The river's water is home to a wide variety of fish, such as paddlefish, drumfish, crappies, trout, and catfish.

Paddlefish are bizarre-looking, sharklike fish that are named for their wide snouts, which look like long paddles. Scientists believe that the snout contains a sense organ that detects the tiny floating plants and animals, called plankton, that the fish feed on.

Below: *A paddlefish's flattened snout not only helps the fish find food, but it also keeps the animal steady while it swims.*

3 Life along the River

From bison hunters to oil fields to race riots, the Arkansas River has been home to many interesting people and witnessed many of the events that have made the United States what it is today.

Below: *A group of Arapaho rest at their camp near Dodge City, Kansas, in 1870. They are drying bison meat on a line.*

Before Europeans arrived, only a few Native peoples lived beside the Arkansas River, and most of them lived along the stretch close to the river's mouth, in what is now Arkansas. The majority of these Natives belonged to Caddo, Osage, and Quapaw groups. Farther upstream, where the river flows across the rolling prairie through what is now Kansas and Colorado, people were few and far between. This was because the treeless prairie was very dry, and its soil was too shallow to be useful for growing crops.

Let's Ride!

This changed when Spanish and French explorers arrived in the sixteenth century, bringing horses with them. Native people had never seen horses, which were new to North America. As European settlers began to take over the land of Native people east of the Mississippi River, many Native groups headed

west to make a life on the prairies, including those beside the Arkansas River. Groups such as the Comanche, Arapaho, and Cheyenne became skilled horse riders and learned to hunt bison that roamed the area in vast herds. They roasted the bison meat over a fire, before drying it into jerky or pounding it into a paste. Bands of Native people lived in tentlike shelters called tepees. These were made from bison skins, as were their clothes and bedding.

DODGING BULLETS IN THE WILD WEST

Perhaps the most famous "wild west" town, Dodge City, Kansas, was once an important cattle-trading post on the Arkansas River. In the late nineteenth century, cowboys drove herds of cattle north from Texas to Dodge City. The animals were loaded onto trains and shipped east to be slaughtered and sold.

Dodge City had many gunmen living there. Law officers, such as Wyatt Earp and Bat Masterson, became famous for their part in that city's history. The many gunmen that died in shoot-outs on the town's streets were buried with their boots on in Boot Hill Cemetery. Historic Boot Hill is now preserved in downtown Dodge City (above).

European Land
The first Europeans to see the Arkansas River were Spanish explorers commanded by Francisco Vasquez de Coronado. His group arrived in southern Kansas in 1541. They had traveled up from what is now Mexico in search of gold but had to return home empty-handed. A few months later, another

Above: *Rene-Robert Cavalier de la Salle claims the territory of Louisiana, which includes the Arkansas River, for France in 1682.*

hundred years. In 1682, French pioneer Rene-Robert Cavalier de la Salle claimed the Arkansas River for France as he created Louisiana—a French territory along the length of the Mississippi River.

Early Settlements

In 1686, at the mouth of the Arkansas River, Henri de Tonty, de la Salle's assistant, founded the first European town in the Louisiana territory. Poste Aux Arcansas (now called Arkansas Post) was built thirty-two years before New Orleans, Louisiana, was founded in 1718 at the mouth of the Mississippi. By 1718, Arkansas Post was the center of a large colony administered by a French company. The colony had attracted thousands of settlers, but the company collapsed in 1720, and many of the colonists went back to France or moved down to New Orleans.

The settlers knew little about the Arkansas River except for the fertile land near its mouth. In 1704, French soldiers had established a camp at Petit Roche (French for "little rock"), where the Arkansas state capital of that name stands today. The mountains and prairies beyond, however,

Spanish explorer, Hernando de Soto, traveled up the Arkansas River from the Mississippi to where the city of Little Rock, Arkansas, stands today.

No other European is recorded as having visited the river for another one remained unexplored by Europeans for many more years. In 1763, control of the western part of the Louisiana territory, including the Arkansas River, was handed from France to Spain, and Britain took over the territory east of the Mississippi River.

War and Peace

During the Revolutionary War (1775–1783), in which Americans fought for their independence from Britain, most of the battles took place in the eastern part of the country. The Colbert Incident, however, was a skirmish that took place at Arkansas Post in 1783. This small battle was the only one to take place west of the Mississippi River, which was still Spanish territory. A pro-British force attacked the town's fort but was repelled by Spanish and Quapaw fighters.

In 1800, France took back control of the land west of the Mississippi. Two years later, Jean Pierre Chouteau, a French trader, traveled up the Arkansas River into what is now Oklahoma and set up a town there.

Below: *Native and non-Native families gather for Sunday school at a church in Indian Territory in 1900. In 1907, Indian Territory became the state of Oklahoma.*

DARK HISTORY OF OIL CITY

Tulsa, Oklahoma, is built on the site of a Creek settlement. It was founded in the late nineteenth century and became a small cowboy town, with fewer than two thousand residents. In 1901, oil was discovered nearby, and Tulsa began to grow. By 1930, Tulsa was home to nearly 150,000 people and had become the "Oil Capital of the World."

Attracted by its newfound wealth, thousands of African Americans came to work in the city during this boom. In 1921, however, the city witnessed one of the worst race riots in U.S. history. Crowds of blacks and whites clashed outside the courthouse over the arrest of a young black man who allegedly attacked a white woman. The black Tulsans were forced to flee under gunfire, and throughout that night, their homes were burned and looted. More than eight hundred people were injured and almost three hundred people died.

Below: *Soldiers take injured prisoners to the hospital after the Tulsa race riot.*

U.S. Territory

In 1803, the United States bought most of France's North American land. This deal was called the Louisiana Purchase, and the French land cost the Americans fifteen million dollars. In 1819, the Arkansas Territory was formed, and it included most of the river. By this time, Arkansas Post, the capital of the territory, was a thriving town. Farther upstream, trading posts, such as Fort Smith and Three Forks (near where Muskogee, Oklahoma, is today), were being set up. In 1821, the territory's

capital was moved upriver to Little Rock, and the following year, steamboats began to make regular journeys up and down the Arkansas River as far as Fort Smith.

In 1830, the United States' government began to move Native people living east of the Mississippi River to unsettled western parts of the Arkansas Territory—into what is now Oklahoma and Kansas. This area was renamed Indian Territory.

Thousands of Native people, mainly Chickasaws, Creeks, and Choctaws from Tennessee and Alabama, were forced to travel down the Arkansas River on flatboats to new locations in the west. The Cherokee were also resettled in northeastern Oklahoma, near present-day Tulsa. They called the journey to this area the Trail of Tears, because they were forced to move in the winter, and thousands of them died from starvation.

Taking the Plains

By the 1850s, non-Native pioneers were being allowed to settle in Kansas, on lands previously reserved for Native groups. At the time, the United States was in an uproar over slavery. People in the north wanted to ban the owning of slaves, while

Above: *Union warships protected with iron plates attack the Confederate force at Arkansas Post in 1863. This was the last battle to take place on the Arkansas River.*

those in the south wanted to be allowed to keep slaves. It was decided that Kansas would become a state, and its residents would be asked to decide if slavery would be allowed there. Settlers from both the north and south arrived and began fighting over whether or not to allow slavery in their new state. Kansas became a free state.

A few weeks after Kansas became a state, the Civil War (1861–1865) began. Southern Confederate troops built Fort Hindman near Arkansas Post to guard the river. In 1863, a Union force destroyed the fort and took control of the river.

The slaves were freed, and the Union won the war. Thousands of these newly freed people and many ex-soldiers moved to Kansas. In the 1870s, a railroad was built through Kansas, heading to New Mexico. The city of Wichita grew up where the railroad met the Arkansas River.

River Traffic

In 1870, only 300 tons (272 tonnes) of cargo were carried on the Arkansas River. The river was too shallow most of the year for many steamboats to travel on it, especially past Fort Smith. No steamboat had

Below: *A man sits on a mountain of bison hides at Dodge City in 1878. During this period, hunters killed hundreds of thousands of bison and almost wiped them out completely.*

ever traveled beyond Fort Gibson, near Muskogee in Oklahoma.

In 1878, the *Aunt Sally*, a large steamer, managed to make the journey from Little Rock all the way to Arkansas City, Kansas. Many more boats began to make this journey, collecting flour and grain produced on the plains of Kansas. However, the river was filled with sandbars and was often too shallow for cargo boats to make regular journeys. Railroads soon took over as the main means of transportation in the region.

Modern Developments

In the 1890s, water from the Arkansas began to be used for irrigating thousands of square miles (sq km) of prairie. In the twentieth century, irrigation projects used even more river water, and a series of dams created several reservoirs, many in the hills of Oklahoma. The dams also helped make the river easier for large barges to navigate. In 1970, the work was completed, making it possible for large cargo ships to travel from Tulsa's port of Catoosa all the way to the Mississippi River and beyond.

PUEBLO

Fort Pueblo, Colorado, was first founded by trappers in the 1840s, where the Arkansas is joined by the Fountain River. The trappers caught furred animals, such as beavers and foxes, in the Rocky Mountains and traded with the local Ute people.

Later, gold prospectors settled on the same site, naming their home Fountain City. This town became the city of Pueblo again in 1860. Pueblo soon became an important producer of steel, and every August since 1872, the city has held the Colorado State Fair.

Above: *Main Street, Pueblo, Colorado, crowded with people in 1910.*

4 Farms and Factories

After centuries as a quiet backwater, the Arkansas River is now at the center of things. Its farms are the most productive in the United States, and its cities produce rockets and jet airplanes.

Below: *A combine works its way through a huge wheat field in Kansas.*

The Arkansas River flows mainly through fields and ranch land, and agriculture is very much the main industry along its course. The river does flow through some big cities, however, such as Wichita, Kansas, and Tulsa, Oklahoma, as it journeys to the Mississippi River. These cities grew up as transportation centers and oil towns. Today, they are home to high technology industries that make rockets and airplanes.

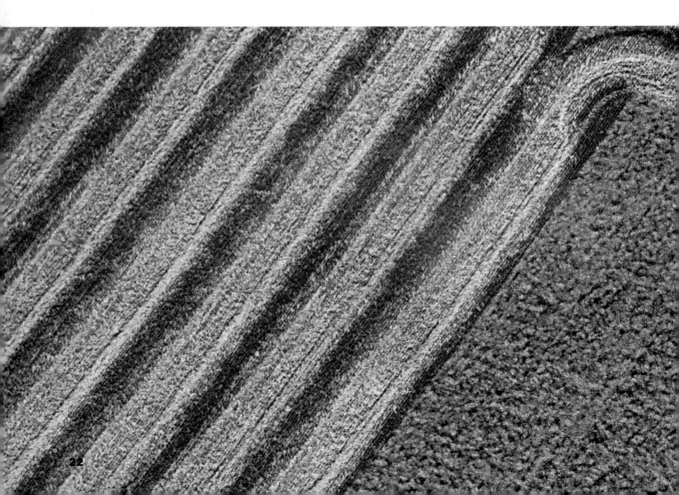

Soil and Water

The final stretch of the Arkansas flows across part of the wide floodplain of the Mississippi River. Over many years of flooding from both rivers, the soil in this region has been enriched by river sediment and is very good for farming. Nearly half of the income of the state of Arkansas comes from agriculture. The state's farms produce more rice than any other U.S. state, while soybeans, cotton, and wheat are other successful crops grown in the region.

To the west beyond the Ouchita Mountains, the land

Main image:
A dam on the Arkansas River holds back floodwater to prevent damage downstream.

beside the Arkansas River is much drier, forming part of the treeless grasslands of the Great Plains. Over the last one hundred years, water from the Arkansas and its tributaries has been used to irrigate the land, especially in Kansas and Oklahoma. Thanks to this irrigation water, crops such as wheat and rye can be grown on the plains.

Depression

In Kansas, however, the land closest to the river's banks is very sandy, which is not

RIVER NAVIGATION SYSTEM

In 1905, the Arkansas Navigation Company was established to find ways to make transportation on the river easier, especially for carrying oil from Tulsa and the Indian Territory (as Oklahoma was named then).

The Arkansas River was very shallow in parts, and dredging deeper channels only worked for a short while because the river soon filled the channels with more silt. In 1954, Professor Hans Einstein (the son of physicist Albert Einstein) was asked to find a solution to this problem. He found that making the river narrower would increase the speed of the current and stop it from silting up.

For the next twenty years, a series of dams, locks, and straightened channels was constructed, and by 1971, the Arkansas River formed a deep channel from the Mississippi to Catoosa—the port of Tulsa on the Verdigris River in Oklahoma. More than eight thousand barges carry 12 million tons (10 tonnes) of cargo on the system each year, most of it to Catoosa, which is the farthest inland, ice-free port in the United States. In 1986, a ship sailed all the way from Germany to Catoosa, the first international ship to travel the entire system.

ideal for growing crops. In the drought of the 1930s, this land was overused, and it turned to dry dust and blew away, creating "dust bowls." The farmers could not make a living from the land, and many thousands of families from Kansas and Oklahoma moved to other parts of the country looking for work. This period was part of the Great Depression, when people from all over the United States and Europe could not find work.

Artificial Lakes

Since those days, dams have been built to store water in reservoirs so crops can be irrigated even in times of drought. The river system's largest reservoirs are in the

Below: *Eufaula Lake in Oklahoma is fed by the Canadian River, a large tributary of the Arkansas.*

mountains of Oklahoma. These artificial lakes collect water from tributaries of the Arkansas, such as the Canadian River. Lake water is run through dams that use the current to make electricity. Lake water is also often emptied into the Arkansas River itself to keep its channels deep enough for boat traffic and to clear away sandbanks.

City Living

The Arkansas River passes through several cities on its route. Pueblo, Colorado, is the first major urban center on the river and is one of the largest in the state. The city has been producing steel for more than 120 years. Many people still work in this industry, making steel components for aircraft and automobiles.

Beyond Pueblo, the river flows for hundreds of miles through rural areas with only a few towns. In central Kansas, the river reaches Wichita, another large city. Oil has been a major industry on this part of the Arkansas River since it was discovered there one hundred years ago. Both Wichita, Kansas, and Tulsa, Oklahoma, farther downstream, have grown up as oil towns.

Below: *Workers gather outside a hanger at the Raytheon plant in Wichita with one of the planes built there.*

Today, only a little oil is pumped out of the ground in the area, but both cities have become important centers for making high-technology products. Wichita is called the "Air Capital of the World" because its factories make more aircraft components than anywhere else in the world. Tulsa, which is the largest city on the Arkansas River, also has factories that make parts for passenger aircraft and warplanes. Rockwell, a Tulsa company, makes rockets used to launch spacecraft and satellites.

In Arkansas, the cities of Fort Smith and Little Rock lie on the Arkansas River.

Little Rock, the state capital, has had a busy river port for 150 years, and today it is still a major transportation center for crops and manufactured products.

HIGH SCHOOL INTEGRATION

In 1957, Central High School in Little Rock, Arkansas, became the focus of race-relations in the United States. The U.S. Supreme Court had ruled in 1954 that segregation—keeping white and black students apart—in public schools was against the Constitution. When the state of Arkansas was ordered to allow African-American students into Central High, Governor Orval E. Faubus sent the Arkansas National Guard to stop the integration. President Dwight D. Eisenhower sent U.S. Army troops to the school to force the state to integrate the school's pupils.

Below: *U.S. soldiers escort African-American students into Central High School on their first day.*

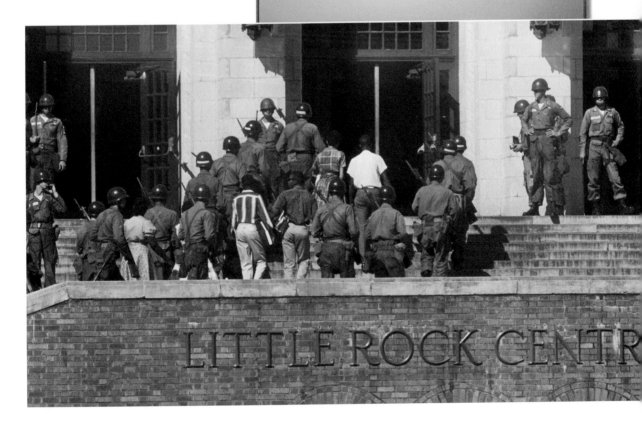

5 Places to Visit

Visitors to the Arkansas River can see many fascinating sites from the early days of the United States, as well as natural wonders from the distant past.

1 Arkansas Headwater Recreation Area, Colorado
Arkansas Headwater Recreation Area covers a 148-mile (237-km) stretch of the river in the foothills of the Rocky Mountains in central Colorado. Visitors can camp by the river in deep canyons among towering mountains.

2 Royal Gorge Route, Colorado
This mountain railroad takes a 12-mile (19-km) route through the Royal Gorge (below), following the river beneath the towering cliffs. Passengers can eat on the train and enjoy the scenery from an observation car.

3 NORAD, Colorado
NORAD is the North American Aerospace Defense Command. Its purpose is to track aircraft and objects in space. The command center is deep inside Cheyenne Mountain.

4 Santa Fe Trail Center, Kansas
The Santa Fe Trail was a popular route between Independence, Missouri, and Santa Fe, New Mexico. Before the

railroads were built, the trail was an important trade route. The center has exhibits showing what life on the trail was like.

❺ Sequoyah's Cabin, Oklahoma

Sequoyah was a Cherokee who developed the first alphabet for his people's language. He lived in Oklahoma in 1828. He worked to reunite the Cherokee after they were forced to leave their homeland in Tennessee. He died in Mexico in 1843, while looking for a lost band of Cherokee people.

Below: *A tunnel is dug through solid rock at NORAD.*

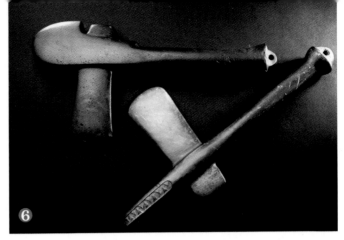

Above: *These stone axes found at Spiro Mounds were used in religious ceremonies.*

❻ Spiro Mounds, Oklahoma

This large site near the Arkansas River has twelve burial mounds built by Native people from 850 to 1450. Spiro was an important center of commerce. The Spiro leaders controlled trade between the open plains to the west and the fertile woodlands to the southeast.

❼ Fort Smith National Historic Site, Arkansas

This site honors Isaac Parker, the "Hanging Judge," who brought law and order to the frontier during the late nineteenth century from his courtroom in Fort Smith. He sentenced 160 men to death in twenty-eight years.

❽ Hot Springs National Park, Arkansas

For more than four thousand years, these naturally hot springs have been thought to have healing qualities. They were also a favorite meeting place of Native people who came here to hunt, trade, and bathe. The Hot Springs were a neutral zone, where fighting between warring groups was not allowed.

❾ Pine Bluff, Arkansas

The city of Pine Bluff was home to the Quapaw people until 1824. This Native group was based on a high, forested bluff above the Arkansas River that was protected from floods. During the Civil War, Arkansas belonged to the Confederacy, which wanted to keep slavery. The residents of Pine Bluff broke away from the rest of the state by supporting the antislavery Union.

❿ Arkansas Post, Arkansas

The site of the first town to be built by European settlers west of the Mississippi River is now protected by the National Parks Service. The area has been flooded by the river many times over the years.

ILLINOIS

MISSOURI

Sequoyah's Cabin

❺ ❼

❻ Fort Smith

ARKANSAS

TENNESSEE

iro
unds

Hot ❽
Springs

❾

Pine Bluff

❿

Arkansas
Post

MISSISSIPPI

How Rivers Form

Rivers have many features that are constantly changing in shape. The illustration below shows how these features are created.

Rivers flow from mountains to oceans, receiving water from rain, melting snow, and underground springs. Rivers collect their water from an area called the river basin. High mountain ridges form the divides between river basins.

Tributaries join the main river at places called confluences. Rivers flow down steep mountain slopes quickly but slow as they near the ocean and gather more water. Slow rivers have many meanders (wide turns) and often change course.

Near the mouth, levees (piles of mud) build up on the banks. The levees stop water from draining into the river, creating areas of swamp.

❶ **Glacier:** An ice mass that melts into river water.

❷ **Lake:** The source of many rivers; may be fed by springs or precipitation.

❸ **Rapids:** Shallow water that flows quickly.

❹ **Waterfall:** Formed when a river wears away softer rock, making a step in the riverbed.

❺ **Canyon:** Formed when a river cuts a channel through rock.

❻ **Floodplain:** A place where rivers often flood flat areas, depositing mud.

❼ **Oxbow lake:** River bend cut off when a river changes course, leaving water behind.

❽ **Estuary:** River mouth where river and ocean water mix together.

❾ **Delta:** Triangular river mouth created when mud islands form, splitting the flow into several channels called distributaries.

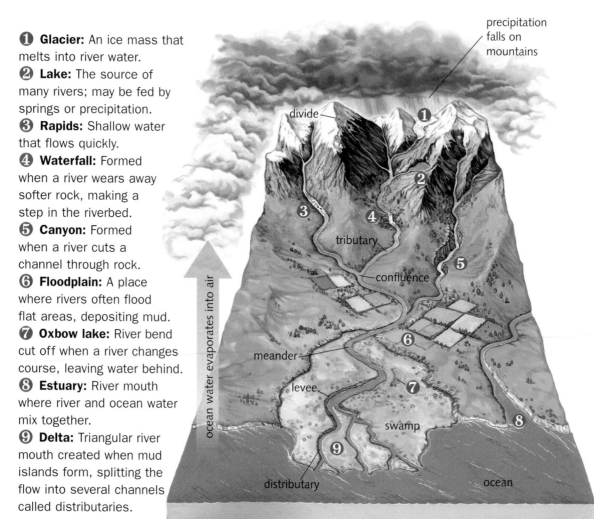

precipitation falls on mountains

divide

tributary

confluence

ocean water evaporates into air

meander

levee

swamp

distributary

ocean

Glossary

agriculture The practice of growing crops and raising livestock as an industry.

basin The area drained by a river and its tributaries.

cargo Transported products or merchandise.

colony A group of people that settle in a new territory but remain loyal to their parent country.

confluence The place where rivers meet.

dam A constructed barrier across a river that controls the flow of water.

flatboat A flat-bottomed barge that can travel through shallow water.

gorge A narrow, steep-sided valley or canyon.

irrigation Watering crops with water from a river, lake, or other source.

levee A raised bank along a river that helps prevent flooding.

navigate To travel through water, steering in an attempt to avoid obstacles.

plateau A large and level surface of land that is higher than the land surrounding it.

reservoir An artificial lake where water is stored for later use.

source The place where a river begins.

steel Iron metal mixed with a small amount of carbon and varying amounts of other metals to make it strong or hard wearing.

tributary A small river that flows into a larger river at a confluence.

valley A hollow channel cut by a river usually between ranges of hills or mountains.

For Further Information

Books

Browne, Turner. *The Last River: Life Along Arkansas's Lower White*. University of Arkansas Press, 1993.

Olien, R. *Arkansas*. Capstone Press, 2003.

Parker, Steve. *Eyewitness: Pond and River*. DK Publishing, 2000.

Wukovits, John F. *Wyatt Earp. Legends of the West series*. Chelsea House Publishers, 1997.

Web Sites

Arkansas River Basin
waterknowledge.colostate.edu/arkansas.htm

Civil War in Arkansas
www.civilwarbuff.org/gillett.html

Dodge City
www.americanwest.com/pages/dodge.htm

Mount Elbert
americasroof.com/co.html

Index